Abrupt Edges

David A. Goodrum

𝄢

Bass Clef Books
Cecilia, KY

First Edition

ISBN

979-8-9898478-6-0

$15.00

Cover photo
Abrupt Edges (2006)
Jen Wenn

Bass Clef Books is an imprint of MARZEK Publishing
Mick Kennedy, Publisher

Printed and distributed by
Kindle Direct Publishing

Table of Contents

Road Atlas

Thumb through pages
as if they're mental states
flashing before your eyes.

*

Praise the unpaved.
Consider dead ends your friends.

Race ahead hoping the past
will hold to the speed limit.

*

Sidle up to abrupt edges that hunt for you
drawn by the fear you exude.
Seek switchbacks without guardrails.
Be ready to pay the toll.

*

The pavement ahead may glisten like fluid sky
but this heavenly mirage is a hallucination.

*

Deny the pull of earth whether
your heart's racing up the mountain
carrying no canisters of water or air
or tumbling downhill to dive
into the ocean laden with rocks
and pungent exhaustion.

*

Detach segments of the globe
like a tangerine
to lessen the weight.

Self-Portrait in Stone

Borne from a creek bed   I am ragged rock
    that darkens when water-covered.

A pale rendition   of my future self
    languished   dry on the window sill

        a gray keepsake   token of affection
           purgatory   for swirling dust

    and dreamt of soft ground   mulching
        what is long done and what is left undone.

I've dragged myself   through wet grass
    to clean myself from all matters.

    Now stranded at the stream's edge
        my hand dipped   in roiling snowmelt

    the woodpecker telegraphs
    its message   *you were lost.*

The bees discover   I proffer no pollen.
The leeches   disregard me

    while they hunt toadlets   recently emerged
        before finding the woods' shelter.

My fear is I'll break down   into gravel
    taken into a bird's gizzard

to help grind down hard seeds   and turn
    small   rounded   smoothed   polished.

Dandelion Vivisection

Gather in the spring
before growing bitter with age.

Don't pluck. Rather
pull out whole by the taproot

though be ready to dig feet deep.
Save everything

for, unlike sadness and poetry,
every part is safe to consume.

Like a bee, stretch
structures apart

to expose the nectary.
Let the sharp leaves mature

then break them
to leak a milky juice.

Decapitate flower from stem
then slice in two

and ponder the yellow arrays
like clusters of new thoughts

before they turn to seed
and are blown apart

by even a child's
tender exhalation.

Hands

the left hand is lecherous
    and drags its glove out at night
        in search of a mate

the right is the thief
    of butchered meat
        and fears losing teeth

they like to intertwine
    and raise a stink
        one middle finger at a time

there is also a dream hand that
    receives all the applause
    cheats at church bingo and Roshambo

    can calm an inflamed appendix
        stillbirthed creatures
        lost minds

    repair invalid baptisms
        shreds of humanity
    grip the dire reality of it all

Extremities Reborn

The prodigal feet return home, fifty-two bones
each deserving a kiss from my hands.

The arch sings its lament as the chorus
of slivers work their own way out.

The aching toes thrum in dreams
of skinned and overripe fruit.

After a day of being nailed
like planks to the floor

they wish to be elevated
better yet swaddled

rocked in your lap
then carried from room to room.

Gently now lift
one then both together

float over to the nursery window
and show them off to the awakening world.

Reminding You to be More Vigilant

Don't break bones to make omelets.
Don't squeeze your heart in a citrus hand press.
Don't scissor-kick in tar pits.
Don't wade into recent history without
erasers and a dinner jacket. Remember
the last one alive gets to run naked.
Don't let your desires pass overhead
like clouds where no one on the ground gets wet.
Don't remain defenseless against gelded angels
or veiled devils. Irritants kept in your mouth
won't form pearls. Don't be a whale who forgets
to resurface after hours of hunting. You can only
be borne breech. Don't despair when they crack
your seeds in two to keep you from germinating.
You are coriander and can still sprout.

Separations

I've scattered words on the ground
so that the squirrel in you
has something to save for winter

pressed them into the visible
cracks around door jambs
to keep the hoarfrost at bay

  *

our first words after sunrise
used to split morning light into whirling
bright bands of impossible color

we would sculpt whole conversations
like blocks of marble, wood, clay, ice
and realize the hidden shapes beneath

  *

we began to recycle phrases
rummaging through newspaper stacks
print smearing hands

with the occasional unexpected
wasp in the garden glove finger
or scorpion in the slipper

  *

slight digs, like bark beetles,
attack and strip branches
we once tended together

while we sleep, remnant consonants
and vowels, tucked into a dead snag,
chant together in requiem

Open Valentine

slice my breastbone
unfold my chest wide

loosen my liver from its cage
feed morsels to your raptor

wrap my bypassed heart
in a waxpaper veil

boxed on the nightstand
next to a clock without hands

shave my skull and savor the wafts
of sulfur from burnt locks of hair

let my lungs air out near the window
drain my bile with a rain chain

mix my blood with red maples
my marrow with pearl dye

to paint over your face and eyes
render my stripped carcass

to carrion scavengers
preserve nothing

Mannequin Exposé

If mannequins could, they would dream
of goosebumps, sweat dripping

evaporating, and the blush
of sex, dilated pupils, engorged vessels.

They feel no shame, modesty. Need no
airbrushing, black tape, blurring.

Cold exhibitionists, they are posed
in repose, nakedness on full display,

shoulders slouched and pelvises arched
by others who ask no consent.

Among a murder of mannequins
the guilty can't be picked out of a lineup.

There are no poker tells.
Also, no cravings

for dermal fillers or botulinum toxin
since they are blessed with ageless

complexion, rather than the thousand
tabloid cuts inflicted on live models.

Stuffed with Scud Clouds

My scarlet throat tugs a thread
of eruptions and aftershocks

rib-bruising punches
from a viral squatter

refusing to check out of
my abandoned abode of hope.

I nod off and medicate
repeatedly, eye

random swatches on walls
shifting in corkscrew webs.

A wrinkled ghost
from my future cautions

not to lose track of pills
and unguent timing

nor pull the pillow
too tightly over my face.

Surgeon's Mistake

Not at all like a jazz riff
repeated over and over becoming art.

Not like a yawn that spreads like contagion.
More serious than the Freudian slip eliciting twitters,

the dining etiquette faux pas that quickly quiets a party
even the nicked painting that lowers the auction price.

More like a software bug
that brings the blue screen of death.

Inappropriate for a mouth to whisper *oops*
but time to listen for failing organs hissing *litigate*.

All the Marks I'll See to the End

O floater in my eye, curlicue that darts away

    a wingless bug buzzless in my periphery
      ascending to escape my swiping hand.

    Zigzags across bright sky
      like an ellipsis of miniature migrating birds.

    On my lover a ghostly beauty spot
      that travels with my gaze
        from her face to chest, thigh and foot.

    *

O mundane scars

    The white patch from a skinned knee
      picked clean of scab in childhood.

    Teenage acne craters
      more recently camouflaged by wrinkles.

    A staple-stamped incision . . .
      beneath its dashes, mesh holding
        my weakened guts in check.

    *

O body constellations

Probed yearly by an orbit of physicians,
    my aging universe continues its trajectory:

      Connecting the astronomical count of dots –
        brown moles, skin tags, cherry angiomas

      —reveals the sagging Hunter on my torso,
      Mild Boar nearby, misshapen
        Horned Goat below.

Cremation Unbound

The dead are piling up
in backlogs.

The crematoriums are stepping up,
answering the angels' call

for the dying to get lit
after viral New Year's celebrations.

We usually request those moribund
to pace themselves and their burning desires

and keep their fervor to ignite tightly bundled
rather than spark our grief's tinder.

But we can't refuse the refuse
of the departed. Their remains remain

and must be burned to dust
at unregulated levels, allowing

proud death to freely disperse
its haughty airs and heated retorts.

The Priest's Last Confession

I no longer listen when stuck in the booth.
I've learned that lending an ear to sins
makes no mortal difference.

I've landed where in the beginning
I had no earthly desire to sit. As if
spewed from a volcano

first cooled pumice, in due course
ground to sand. Why at five,
wanting to please, did I ever say

when I grow up, I want to be a pastor.
Why not geologist or journalist or sailor?
I still feel something when posing questions

like *When was your last confession?*
Questioning is my substitute for sex. I ask,
crave a cigarette and try not to fall asleep.

I always pay attention
to my bones as they wax and wane
across the surface of my rectory single bed

a crucifix from childhood hanging overhead.
I hear my joints creak and swell
like boat sails blown off course

while the persistent mumblings of penitents
contrite, crying and out of breath
sound like flatus in this tiny box.

Advice Over Old Fashioneds

Rye, sugar, bitters, garnish. Named
in the 1880s. Classic. All through a visit,
drinks smooth your path through chats
often populated with potholes, ruts.
Like frozen clusters of white bubbles
trapped inside ice cubes, opinions about
religion politics sex crystalize then
are handed down through generations.

Like when you rant about sorrows
long settled to the bottom, the sunk
steppingstones of broken marriages, greedy
kids, demanding widowed girlfriends,
and the repeating dream that jolts you
awake where they all are yelling
at your lack of sensitivity.

Have you failed to craft sweetness?
For balance you might've aspired to mix
your own raw sugar into simple syrup
by gently heating until the rough granules
dissolve in water, then embraced the hint
of molasses, the music of Turbinado, Demerara.

The unkept secret of your Old Fashioned remains
you doubling down on the bitters, base spirits
infused with tinctured herbs, roots, bark.
Early medicines, and like yourself, now feeling
outdated and best in small doses.

The Least Worry

Bottles
      in the back seat
           levitate
while the driver's
         relaxed feet
             lift up
from pedals.
       Palms float
           off the wheel
failing
     to control
        momentum as he
can't negotiate
      his way out of the curve.

His trajectory is aligned
        with a home's front entry
        and is aiming to land on
        the living room sofa.
But the front yard
canopy tree
     blocking
        moonlight
abruptly denies
      his forward motion.
His car is no gymnast
    and has no twisting reflex
     to stick the landing
      undamaged.

Neighbors, urged by smoke
          curling
from the undercarriage,
       drag him
      from the driver's seat
    as he pukes out a slurred request
   to switch his empties to the trunk.

Monday Night Bashing

His collapsed esophagus
    like a wrung tube sock
        with a knot

and thirteen broken
    ribs   kindling
        for the fire

in the defendants' guts.
Who claim   he'd flashed
    a chipped-tooth pomegranate grin

        as he bumped   and pawed
            his way   through the local dive
      and still waved farewell

        with heel-bruised hands
    when they left the club   and thumped
  across the bridge back into town.

By Wednesday his body   rebroke
    the surface   of a quiet lake channel
        bubbling up like a last

        trace of gas
    from the bottom
of a murky beer glass.

Note the settled blood
    the fading   rigor mortis
        the final relaxation;

    report the search   of his pockets
        finding a marble   resembling
      the eye of a trout,

    the weighing down
        of his lids with coins;
  timestamp the arranged last ride.

Wander by
    the abandoned easement
        where wreckage   washes up

to glimpse   his abandoned cabin
        flaking paint   tilted
            by termites

        window frames   lined
            with glass shards
        tall grass   littered

            with crushed cans   cut
        fishing line   collected
    among the water weeds.

Road Trip

Amber traffic lights whisper *Speed up.*
You can make it. Get out of town.

I whip by fields of spiked canola flowers
poised to become pale gold oil.

Mesmerized by the air wake shaking
creamy meadowfoam buds surviving drought

by lifeless stacked square bales
quiet monuments of harvest

by large rounds of hay wrapped in white
like giant marshmallow

headstones dotting fallow fields.
Setting through pillowed clouds, the sun fades

and then a last flash of yellow rays.
From the overpass ahead a huge truck tire

plummets in the glare, bouncing
on pavement, swooping out of sight

crashing on the moonroof
impaling it into the passenger

seat.
I can't turn to face the horror

of my wife disfigured, paralyzed
or crushed dead

before I realize, I'm driving alone
getting away from it all.

E'ville Awash

E'ville lounges on an oxbow crescent of the Ohio like an incontinent old man. Bakes in the summer, never warm in winter. Never glacier-covered, though left with blankets of voluminous outwash and yellow-brown loess in the valley. Served up dead center on the North American Plate after the breakup of Pangaea. Once lay near the equator, covered by a shallow sea filled with clams, snails, flower-like crinoidea, layer upon layer of invertebrate death, accumulating muck of millennia, solidified into graveyard bedrock. E'ville rests near the remains of Mound Builders of Mississippian culture, land later bought by a family of Angels; shooed away Shawnee from the confluence with Pigeon Creek; hid slaves in the underground railroad; segregated blacks within Governor Street, Canal Street, Lincoln Avenue; birthed the Indiana Klan. E'ville fears decrepitude, insignificance, abandonment, and floods. Like the one in '37 covering 40% of the locale, cutting off all ways to flee: auto, rail, and air. With the 2nd world war boom, whole blocks of houses bloomed up from flat farmland in a single season. Houses in checkerboard rows overflowing during freak summer storms. Parents yelling at kids *Get out of the street!* surging with fetid water. Sewers backing up through the kitchen sink onto counters and floors. In basements, after the cement around posts burst, pushed out by groundwater rising, this scent: Worn-out tractor tire, rotting catfish, pig stink, burnt corn stalk, fermented soybeans.

To My Four-Year-Old Self

Child, take some initiative.

As soon as possible, you should
dress yourself. Here's all you need
to know: Tag in back.

Stop waiting for your busy mother
to wipe your butt, and perhaps avoid
future hemorrhoids.

Start brushing your own teeth
and avoid that bitter day
when she was rushed and haggard

and instead of toothpaste grabbed
your older brother's acne cream.
Don't wear your underwear and socks

to bed; they may keep you warm
but your father will just call you *stinky*.
In fact, soon ask to do your own laundry;

and since they'll end up that way,
prefer gray clothes. Stick
with your swimming lessons.

Not because mother claims if you're on
a capsized boat you'll drown. Nor because
she won't let you go to summer camp

because she's afraid you'll drown.
Nor because she only lets you bathe
in an inch of water, for you might drown.

But because it gets you out of the house.

When Mother Gets Angry

Watch out for whirling debris –
   the dirty dishes
      you left untouched

   unlaundered clothes
      stuffed pets.
Seek immediate shelter

   best in the basement
      with headphones or
  a pillow over your ears

Next best in the bathroom
   nestled in the tub
      door locked

   with the fan and water running.
Hum   happy thoughts
   like when you'll have

      a license job apartment cash.
Avoid getting trapped
   in a car with her

   for your first thought
      may be to open the door
       tuck and roll.

If caught out in the open
   her spinning fingers of clouds
     descending

throw yourself to the ground
   lie flat   don't panic   crawl
     to the closest ditch   ravine   culvert

grovel   duck and cover
     your head with anything   anything at all.

The Dream in Which Mom Says Just Before Dying, *Blink and You Will Miss Me*

I believe you're still asleep
in the next room. Soon you will

shake me awake to deliver
the news to neighbors.

I can't shut my eyes; I can't
keep myself from trying.

I am in a stare-down
with blank walls — pictures

removed though their shadows
remain, shuttered windows, curtains

closed, daylight and moonlight
blocked. No chance of stopping:

The tornado's wail sinking and rising.
The roof tiles' clatter, pelted

by gusts, hail, rain. The prayer plants'
folding in nocturnal devotions. The crests

and troughs of grief. The moment-
to-moment tides of living without you.

Alan's Aftermath

"About the time my mom started calling me by my uncle's
name, she fussed that ceiling lamps flickered, switches turned
on wrong lights, appliances always beeped and the phone

and doorbell constantly rang. She told me she dreamt of
boats gathering outside the front door of her house gutted and
flooded, the refrigerator face-down in the kitchen, doors

unhinged. Do you know someone who would adopt the small
dog that kept my mom company before she passed? I'm
desperate now for a single room lease, unfurnished, no pets.

Immediate occupancy. And do I need a permit for a yard
sale? And do you know where I could dump her last
Christmas tree? Yeah, I know it's March. And I need to

rehome her spayed female cat, Loco, too. Towards the end
she complained of a never-lifting fog, the bright sun shining
through, forming pearly ghost rainbows. And she asked to

have shoelaces removed so tongues could be freed. The last
thing I had said to her was I was just going out for a drive
and at the front door of her rental yelled, *mom, I'll be right*

back! That last morning – that neither of us knew was the
last – after dreaming of St Eligius she pleaded to be re-
baptized in a horse trough. Are there any therapists accepting

new patients? My hair's falling out in handfuls and my skin
is crawling. I want to be hypnotized so that I can stop…
so many things. I know you won't believe me because

everything looks fake to a magician. But I'm seeking dark
sky pointers. Comets are coming and the shaking earth is
spoiling for a fight."

Procrastinations

The weak spring beneath me
as I work to resettle into the cushion.

Tepid green ginger tea in need
of repeated reheating.

Dried apricots—small, flattened
suns for this unwelcomed day.

Assorted crumbs among
crumpled paper wads.

Dried-up ink pens, broken
pencil nibs, worn erasers.

I must do better than a bland
amalgam of stock sorrys

and condolences as solace
for the unexpected grief we share.

Spreading My Cremains

Sift a few at the foot
of my parents' bed
now in the guest room

and beneath the fake stone where
our hidden house key resides
amid landscaped rocks.

Shake some
on the tops of my books
pages sallow and brittle

and already dust covered
with motes of my dead skin, hair
and clothing fibers.

Reunite a few bits with
my shredded diary's ashes
already inurned in the file cabinet.

Add to the bone meal
served to our garden
root vegetables. Make sure

to mix well into the soil
for top dressing can attract
raccoons, coyotes, feral dogs.

Much like the me you know now
my cremains will be best
in moderation, a slow release

like the dandruff I often leave
on your shoulder, where I will
always long to rest my head.

Concrete Memories

A square of bare earth / where a house was.
[...] Concrete stoop.
Two steps up / and you're there.

—Clemens Starck, "Dismantling"

i

steps lead to open
air, the house dismantled
its parts sold off
onsite

concrete remains
will stand my lifetime – and more –
before it all falls apart
less so

if bludgeoned
with a jackhammer

*

fun for others to watch
painful to listen to

do I need such an aggressive tool
for prying into memories

missteps formed within
a frame atop footings
footings poured by parents
and older siblings

*

my childhood home
no longer stands
a chance
once I start to delve

watching silhouettes
shadows, mere outlines

31

from outside
the view obscured
by double pane
glass reflections

      *

who were these people?
bed early and wake early

indiscernible adult goings-on
they come and go
mumbling of backyard grilled chicken
and Jello molds

dad hunched over
a paper spreadsheet
pale green ledger
for a full accounting

numbers in pencil
by hand for me
1¢ for brushing teeth, 2¢
for making the bed, 5¢ each

for collecting house garbage
and hand drying dishes

fudging allowances
for half efforts

      ii

returning after decades
the rooms and furniture

seem worn and small
mom's new toaster oven
in the dining room closet
still unused

all her cooking done
in one crockpot, all cans
in the cupboard expired
dad long passed

but the impression he made
on the easy chair still there

     *

malformed
recollections
retain their bent-
nail shapes

no matter the numbered
attempts to level them out

     *

tempted
to reconstruct?

dig up your old blueprints
faded as they must be
and brush up on surveying skills:
driving stakes to mark territory

much like reading
residues:
damp perk coffee grounds
settled in the cup

dried paint in near-empty buckets
rust stains on porcelain sinks
photo books of sepia
relatives, names written in ink

on top of bodies, faces
faint history in the margins
both things and people
passed on

smudged diaries
illegible letters
bundled into brittle memoirs
by slack rubber bands

pulp fibers
self-consumed by their own acid

iii

if you truly want
access
to cleared air
at the top of empty stairs

first build a door
knock without permission

collect
for childhood chores
delivering news, mowing
yards, taking out the trash

minding
the past's burn pile

*

beg forgiveness
for stolen license plates

clothes reeking of cigarettes
and the roar of the garage door
opening
after curfew

hope you inherit your parents'
tolerance for all the accidents:

scraped knees, broken
collarbones, wrecked cars
exploded pressure cooker
children

Acknowledgments

The author thanks the editors of the following journals in which these works, sometimes in earlier versions and with different titles, first appeared:

Bear River Review: "Advice Over Old Fashioneds" and "E'ville Awash"

Book of Matches: "Hands"

Coffin Bell: "Cremation Unbound"

Death—Lifespan Vol 12 (anthology): "Spreading My Cremains"

Gyroscope Review: "Separations"

I-70 Review: "The Priest's Last Confession"

The Inflectionist Review: "Open Valentine"

Merion West: "Mannequin Exposé"

The San Antonio Review: "To My Four-Year-Old Self, "All the Marks I'll See to the End" and "Reminding You to be More Vigilant"

SHARK REEF Literary Magazine: "The Dream in Which Mom Says Just Before Dying, Blink and You Will Miss Me"

Skylight 47: "Road Trip"

Soup Can Magazine: "Surgeon's Mistake"

Timberline Review: "Extremities Reborn"

Trace Fossils Review: "Alan's Aftermath"

Triggerfish Critical Review: "Monday Night Bashing," "Self-Portrait in Stone" and "The Least Worry"

About the Author

David A. Goodrum, writer/photographer, was born, raised, and educated in Indiana and currently lives in Oregon in the Willamette Valley.

Abrupt Edges is his second chapbook and third publication. Prior books include *Vitals and Other Signs of Life* (The Poetry Box, 2024) and \'spärs(,) pō'et' əkə\ — *Sparse Poetica* (Audience Askew, 2023). Recent poems have appeared in *Tar River Poetry, Gyroscope Review, San Antonio Review, Triggerfish Critical Review, I-70 Review, Cirque, SHARK REEF Literary Magazine, Banyan Review, Skylight 47, Tampa Review,* among others.

David's photography has graced the covers of several art and literature magazines, most recently *Cirque, Willows Wept Review, Blue Mesa Review, Red Rock Review, The Moving Force Journal, Snapdragon Journal, Vita Poetica,* and appeared in many others.

As an undergrad he studied at Indiana University and graduated with a creative writing thesis of poems. He holds degrees in English and German and a doctorate in instructional systems technology. David has been a high school teacher, a developer of instructional software, a fine arts photographer exhibiting at juried art fairs, and a director of educational technology across two different universities.

In fall 2023 he joined the Executive Board of the Oregon Poetry Association and is currently president. He's also been a member of the Board of Directors for The Arts Center in Corvallis since fall 2022.

Find out more about this poet/photographer at www.davidgoodrum.com.